GW00647764

# A Gift for

# ON RAISING CHILDREN

Compiled by
## Mary Hollingsworth

WORD PUBLISHING
Dallas · London · Vancouver · Melbourne

Library of Congress Cataloging-in-Publication Data

    On raising children / compiled by Mary Hollingsworth.
       p.   cm.
    ISBN 0-8499-5030-9
    1. Child rearing—Quotations, maxims, etc.  2. Parenting—Quotations, maxims, etc.  I. Hollingsworth, Mary, 1947–
HQ769.O57  1993
649'.1—dc20                          93–7689
                                            CIP

34569  PLP  9 8 7 6 5 4 3 2 1
*Printed in Hong Kong*

# Of
# Joys and Jolts

Life is a flame that is always burning itself out, but it catches fire again every time a child is born.

*George Bernard Shaw*

The rules for parents
Are but three. . .
Love,
Limit,
And let them be!

*Elaine M. Ward*

*T*he first handshake in life is the greatest of all: the clasp of an infant fist around a parent's finger.

*Mark Beltaire*

*A*h! What would the world be to us
If the children were no more?
We should dread the desert behind us
Worse than the dark before.

*Henry Wadsworth Longfellow*

# Without Children

$W$hat a boring and depressing world this would be without children! Just think, there would be no need for lollipops, cotton candy or licorice. Ponies would be out of work. Amusement parks with carousels would be obsolete. Santa Claus and the Easter Bunny would have to retire. And nobody would care when a baby Robin fell out of its nest.

Infectious giggles would never be heard, and "peek-a-boo" would disappear from the English language. If there were no children, who would make grandparents smile, who would play Patty Cake, and who would try to whistle with crackers in his mouth? Balloons would never pop, milk would rarely spill, and sticky hands from chocolate bars would be a thing of the past.

Without children there would be no use for toy trains, dolls that walk and talk, or Jack-in-the-Box. Barney the Purple Dinosaur would have no one to hug, and Kermit the Frog would just turn green and die. Caterpillars wouldn't get stroked, and turtles would never get to sleep in the house. All in all, life would be a real drag.

Let's face it, children are the essence
of life. They are God's answer to
depression, loneliness, and hate.
Children are joy and love personified.
They are God himself in tiny bodies.

*M.C.H.*

Children are our most valuable
natural resource.

*Herbert Hoover*

Making the decision to have a child
is momentous—it is to decide forever to
have your heart go walking around
outside your body.

*Elizabeth Stone, Village Voice*

# It Will Change Your Life

$\mathcal{T}$ime is running out for my friend. We are sitting at lunch when she casually mentions that she and her husband are thinking of "starting a family. . . ."

"We're taking a survey," she says, half joking. "Do you think I should have a baby?"

"It will change your life," I say carefully, keeping my tone neutral.

"I know," she says. "No more sleeping in on Saturdays, no more spontaneous vacations. . ."

But that is not what I mean at all. I

look at my friend, trying to decide what to tell her. I want her to know what she will never learn in childbirth classes. I want to tell her that the physical wounds of childbearing heal, but that becoming a mother will leave her with an emotional wound so raw that she will be forever vulnerable.

I consider warning her that she will never read a newspaper again without asking, "What if that had been my child?" That every plane crash, every fire will haunt her. That when she sees pictures of starving children, she will look at the mothers and wonder if anything could be worse than watching your child die. I look at her carefully manicured nails and stylish suit and think she should know that no matter how sophisticated she is, becoming a mother will immediately reduce her to the primitive level of a she-bear protecting her cub. That a slightly urgent call of "Mom!" will cause her to drop a soufflé or her best crystal without a moment's hesitation. That the anger she will feel if that call came over a lost toy will be a joy she has never before experienced.

I feel I should warn her that no matter how many years she has invested in her career, she will be professionally derailed by motherhood. She might successfully arrange for childcare, but one day she will be waiting to go into an important business meeting, and she will think about her baby's sweet smell. She will have to use every ounce of discipline to keep from running home, just to make sure he is all right. . . .

Looking at my attractive friend, I want to assure her that eventually she will shed the pounds of pregnancy, but she will never feel the same way about herself. That her life, now so important, will be of less value to her once she has a child. That she would give it up in a moment to save her offspring, but will also begin to hope for more years, not so much to accomplish her own dreams, but to watch her child accomplish his. I want her to know that a cesarean scar or shiny stretch marks will become badges of honor.

My friend's relationship with her husband will change, I know, but not in the ways she thinks. I wish she could understand how much more you can love a man who is careful to always powder the baby or who never hesitates to play "bad guys" with his son. I think she should know that she will fall in love with her husband again for reasons she would now find very unromantic.

I wish my modern friend could sense the bond she will feel with women throughout history who have tried desperately to stop war and prejudice and drunk driving. I hope she will understand why I can think rationally about most issues, but become temporarily insane when I discuss the threat of nuclear war to my children's future.

I want to describe to my friend the exhilaration of seeing your son learn to hit a baseball. I want to capture for her the belly laugh of a baby who is touching the soft fur of a dog for the first time. I want her to taste the joy that is so real that it hurts.

My friend's quizzical look makes me realize that tears have formed in my eyes. "You'll never regret it," I say finally. Then I reach across the table, and squeezing my friend's hand, I offer a prayer for her and me and all of the mere mortal women who stumble their way into this holiest of callings.

*Dale Hanson Bourke*
*Everyday Miracles*

# The Heart of
the Matter

The ability to love is the heart of the
matter.

*Gloria Vanderbilt*

There is something wrong with
our spiritual lives when we do not
love children, and when children
do not love us.

*T. J. Bach*

Children need love, especially when
they do not deserve it.

*Harold S. Hulbert*

If I give love, I inspire and receive love
in return. . . . The wise man loves.

*Ralph Waldo Trine*

# Tiny Teachers

Children are the best teachers in the world. They teach young women how to be mothers and young men how to be fathers. They teach older men and women how to be grandparents. They even teach other children how to be brothers and sisters.

Think about all the skills children teach people. They teach moms how to be nurses and dads how to be heroes. They teach brothers and sisters how to share . . . toys, rooms, dreams, and cookies. They even teach teachers how to teach in creative and fun ways.

Children teach the world how to love. They teach us to look past a person's skin color right to his heart. They teach us how to be honest, open, and innocent. And they teach us how to hug and laugh and be enthusiastic.

Children make us keep our promises because they never forget one that we make. They even make us into scientists and professors by asking "Why?" about every thing that moves and many things that don't.

Isn't it interesting that while we are teaching our children to be adults, they are teaching us how to be children? That's especially important when we remember that Jesus said, "Let the little children come to me. Don't stop them, because the kingdom of heaven belongs to people who are like these children" (Matthew 19:14).

*M.C.H.*

To love others is not enough! Somehow we must make them feel that love, because the only kind of love we can use, is the love we can feel.

*David Jeremiah, Exposing the Myths of Parenthood*

Oh! If only we could learn to "love past" things as children do—wrinkles, warts, handicaps, skin colors, blunderings, cultural differences, a grandparent's funny underwear, and even meanness. Then the world would be a fit place to live.

*M.C.H.*

*I* love preschool children. I love the way they act. I love the way their minds work. I love the freshness with which they approach life. But a toddler . . . can also be extremely frustrating. He harbors a passion to kill things, spill things, crush things, flush things, fall off things, and eat horrible things. Tell me why it is that a toddler will gag over a perfectly wonderful breakfast of ham, eggs, biscuits, juice and jelly. But then he will enthusiastically drink the dog's water and play in the toilet. Truly, he is his mother's greatest challenge . . . and her most inexpressible joy.

*James Dobson, Turn Your Heart Toward Home Films Series*

# Hope for Fathers

The father of a good child is very happy. The person who has a wise son is glad because of him.

*Proverbs 23:22*

# What Is a Father?

*A* father never feels worthy of the worship in a child's eyes. He's never quite the hero his daughter thinks, never quite the man his son believes him to be, and this worries him sometimes. So, he works too hard to try and smooth the rough places in the road for those of his own who will follow him. . . . Fathers are what give daughters away to other men who aren't nearly good enough, so they can have grandchildren who are smarter than anybody's. . . .

*Paul Harvey*

While I don't minimize the vital role played by a mother, I believe a successful family begins with her husband.

*James Dobson*

It sometimes happens, even in the best of families, that a baby is born. This is not necessarily cause for alarm. The important thing is to keep your wits about you and borrow some money.

*Elinor Goulding Smith*

The years are passing so quickly. In a few brief moments, the skateboard will be warped and cracked; the swing-set will be rusty and still; the bicycle tires will be flat; the beds will be unruffled and the halls quiet. We will go through Christmas with no stockings hanging by the fireplace. I understand what is coming and I accept it. . . . But I will say this: when these parenting years have passed, something precious will have flickered and gone out of my life. Thus, I am resolved to enjoy every day that remains in this fathering era.

*James Dobson, Turn Your Heart Toward Home Film Series*

*W*hat a father says to his children is not heard by the world, but it will be heard by posterity.

*Jean Paul Richter*

*A* father is someone who carries pictures where his money used to be.

*Lion*

*O*ne father is more than a hundred schoolmasters.

*George Herbert*
*Outlandish Proverbs*

# Fatherhood

*W*e can never afford to forget that we teach our children to call God "Father," and the only conception of fatherhood that they can have is the conception which we give them. Human fatherhood should be molded and modeled on the pattern of the fatherhood of God. It is the tremendous duty of the human father to be as good a father as God.

*William Barclay*

# Hope for Mothers

*A* mother . . . fills a place so great that there isn't an angel in heaven who wouldn't be glad to give a bushel of diamonds to come down here and take her place.

*Billy Sunday*

*M*other is the name of God in the lips and hearts of little children.

*William Makepeace Thackeray*
*Vanity Fair*

*E*very mother is like Moses. She does not enter the promised land. She prepares a world she will not see.

*Pope Paul VI*
*Conversations with Pope Paul*

*G*od and mothers can fix anything . . . can't they?

*Barbara Johnson*
*Stick a Geranium in Your Hat and Be Happy!*

# A Mother's Promise

*I* will let nothing hurt you,"
She told the child asleep
And wept because the promise
Was one she could not keep.
"But I will never hurt you,"
She said again and wept,
Knowing it a promise
No mortal ever kept.
"Life has deep hurts," she whispered,
"Which no one can avert.
God help me teach you strength and love
For conquering any hurt."

*Jane Merchant*

*A* mother understands what
a child does not say.
*Jewish Proverb*

*T*he mother's heart is the child's
schoolroom.
*Henry Ward Beecher*

*W*hat the daughter does, the
mother did.
*Jewish Proverb*

# Motherhood

What should we do while we wait for society to get its priorities straight? Speaking as a husband, I believe there is much that married men can do in their own homes. First of all, tell your wife you love her. Thank her for being in your home with your children. Let her know that the choices she has made are honored by you. In short, tell her how much she matters!

It isn't too late to restore the fine art of motherhood back to its time-honored position in our society. In spite of the current cultural hostility, lack of support from husbands, and incredible pressures inside and outside the home, women continue to affirm the importance of motherhood.

A Roper poll published in *Ladies Home Journal* reported on a survey of women who were asked to describe the best thing about being a woman today. Sixty percent said it is "motherhood." At least today's pervasive propaganda against bearing and raising children hasn't convinced everyone!

*James Dobson*
*Children at Risk*

*A* mother's love is not blind;
it's just very nearsighted.

*Author Unknown*

*T*o a mother, a son is never a fully
grown man; and a son is never a fully
grown man until he understands and
accepts this about his mother.

*Sydney Harris*

*A* sweater is a garment worn by a
child when his mother feels chilly.

*Barbara Johnson*
*Splashes of Joy in the Cesspools of Life!*

# Fretting

*H*ow many mistakes I have made with the children because I was fretting—concerned to the point of worry. And invariably it prompted me to unwise action: sharpness, unfair punishment, unwise discipline . . . even my attitude and tone of voice.

But a mother who walks with God knows he only asks her to take care of the possible and to trust him with the impossible; she does not need to fret.

*Ruth Bell Graham*
*Prodigals and Those Who Love Them*

# Show
# and Tell

*M*y son, pay attention to me. And watch closely what I do.

*Proverbs 23:26*

The good person who lives an honest
life is a blessing to his children.

*Proverbs 20:7*

Only as genuine Christian holiness and
Christlike love are expressed in the life of a
parent can the child have the opportunity
to inherit the flame and not the ashes.

*Stephen G. Green*

# Teach Me How to Live

*Y*ou taught me lots of things,
Mom—more than any other teacher.
You taught me how to cook and sew,
how to dust and clean and do the
laundry. You taught me how to shop for
groceries and compare prices, how to
plant flowers and even how to "play
second fiddle." And you never got angry
when I learned slowly or made mistakes.
You just patiently started again and
again until I could do it on my own.

   You also taught me the more
important things in life—things that

made life exciting and worthwhile. You taught me it was more blessed to give than to receive by taking cakes to the neighbors. You taught me to love the lonely by visiting the retirement homes and your aging relatives and friends. You taught me the meaning of humility by quietly serving others and taking no credit for yourself. And you taught me kindness by the way you spoke to the mailman, the paperboy and the old man who came to our back door for something to eat. You taught me how to live.

*M.C.H.*

*For Mom with Love*

*M*others give sons permission to be princes, but the fathers must show them how. . . . Fathers give daughters permission to be princesses, and mothers must show them how. Otherwise, both boys and girls will grow up and always see themselves as frogs.

*Eric Berne*

# Role Model

$\mathcal{A}$lbert Einstein was with a group of aspiring young scientists in his laboratory one day, and he decided to give them a lesson, not in physics but in being real men. He pushed his glasses up on his nose, pointed his bony finger, and said, "Gentlemen, try not to become men of success. Rather, become men of value."

That's a great piece of wisdom for every dad to impart to his kids. Instead of pushing your child to become a success, let him or her know that you prefer that they become men or women of value.

And the best way to do that is to show them, not simply tell them. Every dad is the family role model, whether he wants the job or not.

*Dennis Rainey*
*Staying Close*

# On the
# Homefront

$\mathcal{H}$ouses are made of wood and stone,
but only love can make a home.

*Author Unknown*

The best place for a child to learn
religious faith is at home,
in the bosom of a family where
faith is lived and practiced.

*Dick Van Dyke*
*Faith, Hope and Hilarity*

When it comes to parenting, kids
don't bloom and grow if their roots are
constantly ripped out. Insecurity in a
home pulls out roots; security provides
the depth and shelter for them to thrive.

*Gary Smalley and John Trent*
*The Language of Love*

# Home and Haven

*C*ountless times each day a mother does what no one else can do quite so well. She wipes away a tear, whispers a word of hope, eases a child's fear. She teaches, ministers, loves, and nurtures the next generation of citizens. And she challenges and cajoles her kids to do their best and be the best. But no editorials praise these accomplishments.

There are no news stories telling us that today a child was taught what it

means to be loved, an infant was hugged
securely, or that the wonders of the
classics were introduced to a young
mind. No one seems to care that a
house was made a home, or that a
simple table of food was transformed
into a place of community and
nurturing.

*James Dobson*
*Children at Risk*

# Third-Shift Kids

*M*ost homes nowadays seem to be on three shifts. Father is on the night shift; mother is on the day shift; and the children have to shift for themselves.

*Author Unknown*

# Parental Imprints

When Woodrow Wilson was president of Princeton University, he spoke these words to a parents' group:

"I get many letters from you parents about your children. You want to know why we people up here in Princeton can't make more out of them and do more for them. Let me tell you the reason we can't. It may shock you just a little, but I am not trying to be rude. The reason is that they are your sons, reared in your homes, blood of your blood, bone of your bone. They have absorbed the ideals of your homes. You have formed and fashioned them. They are your sons. In those malleable, moldable years of their lives, you have forever left your imprint upon them."

# Can We Talk?

God said, "Remember my words in your hearts and souls. . .Teach them well to your children. Talk about them when you sit at home and walk along the road. Talk about them when you lie down and when you get up. Write them on your doors and gates. Then both you and your children will live a long time in the land."

*Deuteronomy 11:18–21a*

*Could I turn back the time machine, I would double the attention I gave my children and go to fewer meetings.*

*J. D. Eppinga*

Too many parents live with the regrets of abandoned moments. It takes time to be silly, to share a secret, to heal a hurt, to kiss away a tear. Moments of uninhibited communication between child and parent cannot be planned; they just happen. The only ingredient we bring to that dynamic of family life is our availability . . . and that is spelled T-I-M-E.

*David Jeremiah, Exposing the Myths of Parenthood*

# Take the Time

*I*t's nine-fifteen and bedtime took
too long (once again).

Another kiss, another glass of water,
and then—

The questions come . . . the hands
hold tight . . . the eyes are open wide.

And something in me whispers,
"Now's the time . . ."

"Mommy, why did Muffy die?"
"Daddy, where's the sun?"

"Are there cats in heaven?" and
"Why did Jesus come?"

And though a whole day's dishes

wait, and bills are piled high,

    Something in me whispers . . . "Take the time. . ."

CHORUS:

    Take the time while they're right here by your side.

    Take the time while their hearts are open wide.

    Teach them how to love the Lord with all their hearts and minds.

    Oh, they're only home a season . . . take the time!

*Song by a Young Mother*
*Quoted by David Jeremiah*
*Exposing the Myths of Parenthood*

*The first duty of love is to listen.*

Paul Tillich

*A* lasting gift to a child, including grown children, is the gift of a parent's listening ear—and heart. Listen first and talk afterward. Then, instead of saying things that may bruise and cut, your words will be pleasant, like honey, sweet to the soul of your child and healing to your relationship. Talking is sharing . . . listening is caring.

Barbara Johnson
*Splashes of Joy in the Cesspools of Life*

# Tell Me More

The time for training children is during their early years. By the time they reach their teens, we need for the most part to shut up and listen. By that time they know what we expect of them, but they do need a sounding board. It can be inconvenient, especially if the teenager is a night owl, or if they catch you in the middle of an interesting book. Never mind, prop yourself comfortably in bed even if you have to force your eyes open. Put the book down. Stop whatever you are doing.

You're fortunate to have a teenager who wants to talk. Be interested and listen. Don't argue. If you can, ask a question like, "Do you think what you're doing (or thinking of doing) is wise? Would you want your son to do it?" Or just be interested. "Tell me more" will encourage them to talk.

Condensed: Preteens, teach. Teens, listen.

*Ruth Bell Graham*
*Prodigals and Those Who Love Them*

# Listen

When I ask you to listen to me and you start giving advice, you have not done what I asked.

When I ask you to listen to me and you begin to tell me why I shouldn't feel that way, you are trampling on my feelings.

When I ask you to listen to me and you feel you have to do something to solve my problem, you have failed me, strange as that may seem.

So, please listen and just hear me.

And, if you want to talk, wait a minute for your turn; and I'll listen to you.

*Author Unknown*

# Building Blocks of a Relationship

1. **Acceptance** gives your child a sense of security.
2. **Appreciation** gives him or her a sense of significance.
3. **Availability** gives your child a sense of importance and worth.
4. **Affection** builds a sense of lovability.
5. **Accountability** gives a sense of responsibility.

*Josh McDowell*
*How to Help Your Child Say "No" to Sexual Pressure*

# Setting the Limits

Parents who neglect discipline are their children's worst enemies.

*F. Marion Dick*

The thing that impresses me most about America is the way parents obey their children.

*The Duke of Wellington*

Do not handicap your children by making their lives easy.

*Robert Heinlein*

Love must be tough.

*James Dobson*

# Rules and Rebels

When parents try to lay down rules without first establishing a real relationship with their children, the natural result will be rebellion.

Rules without relationship lead to rebellion.

*Josh McDowell, How to Be a Hero to Your Kids*

*The best time to tackle a minor problem is before he grows up.*

Ray Freedman

*It is easier and better to build boys than to repair men.*

Author Unknown

*If discipline was practiced in every home, juvenile delinquency would be reduced by 95 percent.*

J. Edgar Hoover
Former Chief, Federal Bureau of Investigation

# Life or Death Issue

*Y*ears ago a famous children's specialist said, "When it comes to a serious illness, the child who has been taught to obey stands four times the chance of recovery than the spoiled and undisciplined child does."

Has it ever occurred to you that obedience may mean the saving or losing of your child's life?

*Adapted from J. Adam Clark*

$T$here are a great many fathers who tie up their hound dogs at night and let their sons run loose.

*Author Unknown*

$W$hen parents don't mind that the children don't mind, then children don't.

*Author Unknown*

$T$rain a child how to live the right way. Then even when he is old, he will still live that way.

*Proverbs 22:6*

# Pains and Prodigals

*L*ove never fails.

*1 Corinthians 13:8*

*K*ids can be a pain in the neck when they're not being a lump in your throat.

*Quoted in Splashes of Joy in the Cesspools of Life! by Barbara Johnson*

*U*nconditional love is loving a child no matter what. No matter what the child looks like. No matter what his assets, liabilities, handicaps. No matter what we expect him to be, and most difficult, no matter how he acts.

*Ross Campbell*

*If* it was going to be easy to
raise kids, it never would have started
with something called labor.

*Author Unknown*

*A* child today faces more sexual signals and temptations on the way to school than his grandfather did on Saturday night when he went out looking for them!

*Josh McDowell,*
*How to Help Your Child Say "No" to Sexual Pressure*

God loves our children infinitely more than we can, because he is the perfect parent with perfect love. I am able to be with and help my children only to the limit of my presence. But there is no boundary to his presence.

*Lee Ezell*
*Pills for Parents in Pain*

Do not worry about anything, but pray and ask God for everything you need, always giving thanks. And God's peace, which is so great we cannnot understand it, will keep your hearts and minds in Christ Jesus.

*Philippians 4:6–7*

# Bits of Wit
## and Wisdom

The trouble with cleaning the house is that it gets dirty the next day anyway. So, skip a week if you have to. The children are the most important thing.

*Barbara Bush*

Children need your presence
more than your presents.

*Jesse Jackson*

What's done to children, they
will do to society.

*Karl Menninger*

We never know the love of our parents
until we have become parents.

*Henry Ward Beecher*

You can con a con, you can fool a
fool, but you can't kid a kid.

*Josh McDowell*
*How to Be a Hero to Your Kids*

*C*hildren are a great comfort in old age—
and they help you reach it faster, too!

*Lionel M. Kaufman*

*C*hildren seldom misquote you. They
more often repeat word for word what
you shouldn't have said.

*Mae Maloo*

*T*he trouble with being a parent is that
by the time you're experienced, you're
unemployed.

*Kredite News*

*P*arenting, like war, is a lot easier to
begin than it is to end.

*David Jeremiah*
*Exposing the Myths of Parenthood*

*T*he family that stays together
probably only has one car.

*B*e nice to your children . . . they will
someday choose your rest home.

*Lee Ezell*
*Pills for Parents in Pain*

*P*eople who say they sleep like a baby
usually don't have one.

*L. J. Burke*

# A Parent's Prayer

Oh, heavenly Father, make me a better parent. Teach me to understand my children, to listen patiently to what they have to say, and to answer all their questions kindly. Keep me from interrupting them or contradicting them. Make me as courteous to them as I would have them be to me.

Forbid that I should ever laugh at their mistakes, or resort to shame or ridicule when they displease me. May I never punish them for my own selfish satisfaction or to show my power.

Let me not tempt my child to lie or steal. And guide me hour by hour that I may demonstrate by all I say and do that honesty produces happiness.

Reduce, I pray, the meanness in me. And when I am out of sorts, help me, O Lord, to hold my tongue.

May I ever be mindful that my children are children, and I should not expect of them the judgment of adults.

Let me not rob them of the opportunity to wait on themselves and to make decisions.

Bless me with the bigness to grant them all their reasonable requests, and the courage to deny them privileges I know will do them harm.

Make me fair and just and kind. And fit me, oh Lord, to be loved and respected and imitated by my children. Amen.

*Abigail Van Buren*
*"Dear Abby" as quoted in Pastor's Manual*